Instant Kendo UI Mobile

Practical recipes to learn the Kendo UI Mobile library
and its various components for building mobile
applications effectively

Sagar Ganatra

[PACKT]
PUBLISHING

BIRMINGHAM - MUMBAI

Instant Kendo UI Mobile

First published: July 2013

Production Reference: 1190713

Published by Packt Publishing Ltd.
Livery Place
35 Livery Street
Birmingham B3 2PB, UK.

ISBN 978-1-84969-911-2

www.packtpub.com

Credits

Author
Sagar Ganatra

Reviewers
Joe Johnston

David J McClelland

Adi Singh

Acquisition Editor
Kartikey Pandey

Commissioning Editor
Harsha Bharwani

Technical Editor
Zafeer Rais

Project Coordinator
Suraj Bist

Proofreader
Lauren Tobon

Production Coordinator
Aparna Bhagat

Cover Work
Aparna Bhagat

Cover Image
Ronak Dhruv

About the Author

Sagar Ganatra is a frontend architect from Bangalore, India. His expertise include HTML5, CSS3, Object Oriented JavaScript, Kendo UI, jQuery, and JavaScript frameworks such as BackboneJS, RequireJS, and AngularJS. He also writes about these technologies in his blog `http://www.sagarganatra.com/`. When he is not coding, he enjoys writing short stories, swimming, and reading books.

I would like to thank my parents for all that they have done for me.

About the Reviewers

Joe Johnston is a veteran LAMP stack application architect and developer with over fifteen years of experience producing software as a service and traditional desktop applications. He is the co-author of *Programming Web Services with XML-RPC and Unix Power Tools, 3rd Edition, O'Reilly*. He has written for the Perl Journal, IBM's developer Works, and XML.com. His blog is `http://taskboy.com/`.

David J McClelland has been creating cutting-edge software and content that bridges design, development, and information for over 20 years. He is currently a principle user interface engineer, developing software to manage distributed devices via the cloud.

> I would like to thank my family for encouraging my many technical and artistic interests.

Adi Singh is a coder and roboticist from Stanford University with a keen interest in investing, travelling, and swimming. A recipient of the prestigious SIA-Youth Scholarship from the Singapore's Ministry of Education and a McCaw Scholarship from Stanford, he has programmed for many renowned organizations, such as Stanford Space Development Lab, Rolls-Royce Deutschland, and Couchsurfing, in the past.

He took a gap for a year after his Junior college to travel around the world and train himself in professional coding outside an educational environment. He recently completed his latest adventure dubbed *10-countries-in-10-weeks* and keeps busy these days managing his tech firm Hacero Labs. He will be returning back to Stanford this fall to complete his studies.

www.PacktPub.com

Support files, eBooks, discount offers and more

You might want to visit www.PacktPub.com for support files and downloads related to your book.

Did you know that Packt offers eBook versions of every book published, with PDF and ePub files available? You can upgrade to the eBook version at www.PacktPub.com and as a print book customer, you are entitled to a discount on the eBook copy. Get in touch with us at service@packtpub.com for more details.

At www.PacktPub.com, you can also read a collection of free technical articles, sign up for a range of free newsletters and receive exclusive discounts and offers on Packt books and eBooks.

http://PacktLib.PacktPub.com

Do you need instant solutions to your IT questions? PacktLib is Packt's online digital book library. Here, you can access, read and search across Packt's entire library of books.

Why Subscribe?

- Fully searchable across every book published by Packt
- Copy and paste, print and bookmark content
- On demand and accessible via web browser

Free Access for Packt account holders

If you have an account with Packt at www.PacktPub.com, you can use this to access PacktLib today and view nine entirely free books. Simply use your login credentials for immediate access.

Table of Contents

Preface

Kendo UI is a HTML5, jQuery-based framework for building rich web applications. The framework contains a comprehensive set of UI widgets, a data visualization framework, a mobile framework, and several tools that enable you to build rich web applications rapidly. This book provides a set of recipes for building intuitive applications for the mobile platform. The Kendo UI Mobile framework contains several UI widgets and an application framework that enables you to build and configure the mobile applications.

The mobile framework renders the application by providing a native look and feel on various mobile platforms including iOS, Android, and Blackberry. This allows developers to focus on the functionality of the application and rely on the framework to provide a native look and feel.

What this book covers

Downloading Kendo UI Mobile (Simple) helps you download the Kendo UI framework and take a look at the various bundles that are packaged in the framework.

Creating a sample application (Simple) gets us started with the Kendo UI Mobile framework and build a sample application using the same. We will also see some of the Mobile UI widgets, such as layouts, views, navbar, and tabstrip in brief.

Using the Application object to configure the application (Intermediate) helps us understand the core component of the framework, that is, the Application object and how it is used to configure the application.

Adding touch events to your mobile application (Intermediate) explains how the framework handles various touch-based events, such as tap, double-tap, hold, and swipe.

Displaying different types of views on a page (Intermediate) describes how to organize the code by specifying views in different documents (remote views) and refer to the them in the main document. *Specifying view transitions* is a follow up section of this recipe where we will see various transition effects that can be applied when navigating from one view to another.

Adding form elements to a mobile page (Simple) illustrates the various form elements that can be added to the mobile page view.

Creating a list using the ListView widget (Intermediate) explains how to create a list using the mobile framework's ListView widget and perform some actions on the list items.

Showing a list of actions to perform using the ActionSheet widget (Advanced) explains the use of the ActionSheet widget to create a list of actions to be applied on the items in the list.

Displaying a Modal window using the ModalView widget (Advanced) helps us create a modal view window using the Modal View widget.

Creating a TabStrip for a mobile application (Intermediate) revisits the TabStrip widget and creates a tab strip to help you navigate from one view to the other.

Using the ScrollView widget to navigate through the application (Intermediate) helps us create a photo gallery-like application and use the framework's ScrollView widget to scroll through different pictures in the gallery.

Rendering with native look and feel using the adaptive rendering technique (Simple) takes a look at how the mobile framework provides a native look and feel for the application without having the developer to maintain different code base for various platforms.

Handling change in the layout orientation using the automatic layout system (Simple) helps us understand how the framework renders the application when there is a change in the layout orientation.

What you need for this book

This book contains various recipes for building mobile applications using the Kendo UI Mobile framework. You are required to download the framework as mentioned in the first recipe. The Kendo UI Mobile framework has a dependency on the jQuery library and should be included before providing a reference to the Kendo UI Mobile framework.

Basic knowledge in building web applications using HTML, CSS, and JavaScript is required. It will be helpful if you have built mobile applications using the mentioned technologies.

Who this book is for

This book is for web developers looking forward to building mobile applications using HTML, CSS, and JavaScript. It is also for mobile application developers trying to build applications that provide native look and feel on various mobile platforms.

Conventions

In this book, you will find a number of styles of text that distinguish between different kinds of information. Here are some examples of these styles, and an explanation of their meaning.

Code words in text are shown as follows: "We can include other contexts through the use of the include directive."

A block of code is set as follows:

```
<div data-role="tabstrip"
  data-select="selectEvent">
  ....
</div>
```

New terms and **important words** are shown in bold. Words that you see on the screen, in menus or dialog boxes for example, appear in the text like this: "clicking the **Next** button moves you to the next screen".

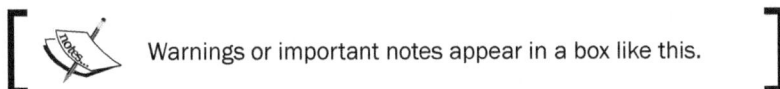

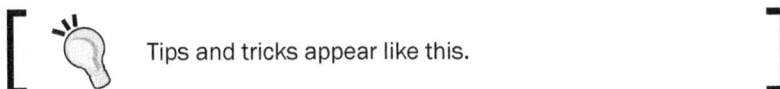

Warnings or important notes appear in a box like this.

Tips and tricks appear like this.

Reader feedback

Feedback from our readers is always welcome. Let us know what you think about this book— what you liked or may have disliked. Reader feedback is important for us to develop titles that you really get the most out of.

To send us general feedback, simply send an e-mail to feedback@packtpub.com, and mention the book title via the subject of your message.

If there is a topic that you have expertise in and you are interested in either writing or contributing to a book, see our author guide on www.packtpub.com/authors.

Customer support

Now that you are the proud owner of a Packt book, we have a number of things to help you to get the most from your purchase.

Downloading the example code

You can download the example code files for all Packt books you have purchased from your account at `http://www.packtpub.com`. If you purchased this book elsewhere, you can visit `http://www.packtpub.com/support` and register to have the files e-mailed directly to you.

Errata

Although we have taken every care to ensure the accuracy of our content, mistakes do happen. If you find a mistake in one of our books—maybe a mistake in the text or the code—we would be grateful if you would report this to us. By doing so, you can save other readers from frustration and help us improve subsequent versions of this book. If you find any errata, please report them by visiting `http://www.packtpub.com/submit-errata`, selecting your book, clicking on the **errata submission form** link, and entering the details of your errata. Once your errata are verified, your submission will be accepted and the errata will be uploaded on our website, or added to any list of existing errata, under the Errata section of that title. Any existing errata can be viewed by selecting your title from `http://www.packtpub.com/support`.

Piracy

Piracy of copyright material on the Internet is an ongoing problem across all media. At Packt, we take the protection of our copyright and licenses very seriously. If you come across any illegal copies of our works, in any form, on the Internet, please provide us with the location address or website name immediately so that we can pursue a remedy.

Please contact us at `copyright@packtpub.com` with a link to the suspected pirated material.

We appreciate your help in protecting our authors, and our ability to bring you valuable content.

Questions

You can contact us at `questions@packtpub.com` if you are having a problem with any aspect of the book, and we will do our best to address it.

Instant Kendo UI Mobile

Welcome to *Kendo UI Mobile*. This book will tell you how to get started with the Kendo UI Mobile framework and also build a sample application using this framework.

Downloading Kendo UI Mobile (Simple)

The Kendo UI Mobile library comes with several widgets and a framework that aids you in building mobile applications quickly. Firstly, you need to download the framework and then include the necessary files in your HTML page.

Getting ready

To download the Kendo UI Mobile framework, navigate to www.kendoui.com and click on the **Download** button. You will be provided with the following five options on the download page:

- **Kendo UI WEB**: It is an open source version that includes components for building applications for the Web. Please note that this does not include the mobile library.
- **Kendo UI Complete for PHP**: A 30-day free trial version of Kendo UI Web, mobile, data-visualization libraries, and server wrappers for PHP.
- **Kendo UI Complete for JSP**: A 30-day free trial version of Kendo UI Web, mobile, data-visualization libraries, and server wrappers for JSP.
- **Kendo UI Complete for ASP.NET MVC**: A 30-day free trial version of Kendo UI Web, mobile, data-visualization libraries, and server wrappers for ASP.NET MVC.
- **Kendo UI Complete**: A 30-day free trial version of Kendo UI Web, mobile, and data-visualization libraries.

How to do it...

It is recommended that you download the free trial version of **Kendo UI Complete** (the last option in the previous list). However, if you prefer any of the server-side programming languages mentioned previously to generate the client-side JavaScript code, you can download the respective option. Now, perform the following steps:

1. Click on the **Download Free Trial** button under **Kendo UI Complete**.

2. You will be required to sign up before downloading the trial version.

3. Once you have signed up, the download page will be shown and an automatic download of files will start immediately.

4. The downloaded ZIP archive will contain the following directories:

    - `/examples`: A set of examples for the Kendo UI Web, mobile, and data visualization

    - `/js`: A set of minified JavaScript files

    - `/css` or `/styles`: A set of minified CSS files

    - `/vsdoc`: The completion helper for Visual Studio 2008 SP1 or newer

    - `/license-agreements`: This contains the license agreement documents

    - `Changelog.html`: This contains the release notes

    - `README`: This contains the readme document

You can run the applications that have been built using this library, which can be found in the `examples` directory. In the next recipe, we will see how you can build a sample application using the Kendo UI Mobile library.

Creating a sample application (Simple)

A Kendo Mobile application is built using HTML5, CSS, and JavaScript. The framework provides JavaScript and CSS files that should be included in your project. A Kendo mobile application can be viewed as being made up of two pieces – the framework and a set of widgets. The framework provides core functionality such as loading views, managing application history, and navigation. The widgets allow you to add visual elements to the page and Kendo UI Mobile comes with several of them that aid you in building the application.

How to do it...

To create an application, include the JavaScript and CSS files in your page. Perform the following steps:

1. Create an HTML document, `index.html`, under your project directory. Please note that this directory should be placed in the web root of your web server.

2. Create the directories `styles` and `scripts` under your project directory.

3. Copy the CSS file `kendo.mobile.all.min.css`, from `<downloaded directory>/styles` to the `styles` directory created in step 2. Then add a reference to the CSS file in the head section of the document.

4. Download the jQuery library from `jQuery.com`. Place this file in the scripts directory and add a reference to this file in the document before closing the body tag. You can also specify the CDN location of the file in the document.

5. Copy the JavaScript file `kendo.mobile.min.js`, from the `<downloaded directory>/js` tag to the `scripts` directory created in step 2. Then add a reference to this JavaScript file in the document (after jQuery).

6. Add the text "Hello Kendo!!" in the body tag of the `index.html` file as follows:

```
<!DOCTYPE HTML>
<html>

  <head>
    <title>My first Kendo Mobile Application</title>
    <link     rel="stylesheet"
    type="text/css"
    href="styles/kendo.mobile.all.min.css">
  </head>

  <body>
    Hello Kendo!!

    <script type="text/javascript"
    src="scripts/jquery.min.js">
    </script>
    <script type="text/javascript"
    src="scripts/kendo.mobile.min.js">
    </script>
  </body>

</html>
```

The preceding code snippet is a simple HTML page with references to Kendo Mobile CSS and JavaScript files. These files are minified and contain all the features, themes, and widgets. In production, you would like to include only those that are required. The downloaded ZIP file includes CSS and JavaScript files for specific features. However, in development you can use the minified files that contain all features.

Another thing to note is that apart from the reference to the script kendo.mobile.min.js, the page also includes a reference to jQuery. It is the only external dependency for Kendo UI.

When you view this page on a mobile device, you will see the text **Hello Kendo!!** shown. This page does not include any of the widgets that come as a part of the library. Now let's build on top of our Hello World application and add some visual elements; that is, UI widgets to the page. This can be done with the following steps:

1. Add a layout first. A mobile application generally has a header, a footer, and multiple views. It is also observed that while navigating through different views in an application, the header and footer remain constant. The framework allows you to define a global layout that may contain a header and a footer for all the views in the application. Also, the framework allows you to define multiple views that can share the same layout. The following is the same page that now includes a header and footer defined in the layout:

```
<body>

<div
  data-role="layout"
  data-id="defaultLayout">

  <header data-role="header">

    <div data-role="navbar">
      My first application
    </div>

  </header>
  <footer data-role="footer">
```

```
    <div data-role="tabstrip">
      <a data-icon="about">About</a>
      <a      data-icon="settings">Settings</a>
    </div>

  </footer>

</div>

</body>
```

2. The body contains a few `div` tags with data attributes. Let's look into one of these tags in detail.

   ```
   <div data-role="layout" data-id="defaultLayout">
   ```

   Here, the `div` tag contains two data attributes, `role` and `id`. The `role` data attribute is used to initialize and configure a widget. The `data-role` attribute has a value, `layout`, identifying the target element as a `layout` widget. All the widgets are expected to have a `role` data attribute that helps in marking the target element for a specific purpose. It instructs the library which widget needs to be added to the page. The `id` data attribute is used to identify the widget (the `layout` widget) in the page. A page may define several layout widgets and each one of these must be identified by a unique ID. Here, the `data-id` attribute has `defaultLayout` as its value. Now there can be many views referring to this layout by its id (views are explained in the next recipe and in detail in the later ones).

3. Similarly, there are other elements in the page with the `data-role` attribute, defining them as one of widgets in the page. Let's take a look at the `header` and `footer` widgets defined inside the layout.

   ```
   <header data-role="header">... </header>
   <footer data-role="footer">...</footer>
   ```

   The header and footer tags have the `role` data attribute set to `header` and `footer` respectively. This aligns them to the top and bottom of the page, giving the rest of the available space for different views to render. Also, note that there is a `navbar` widget in the header and a `tabstrip` widget defined in the footer. As mentioned earlier, the framework comes with several widgets that can help you build the application rapidly. The usage of `navbar`, `tabStrip`, and many other widgets will be covered in the later recipes of this book.

4. Now add views to the page. The `index.html` page now has a layout defined and when you run the page in the browser, you will see an error message in the console which says:

   Uncaught Error: Your kendo mobile application element does not contain any direct child elements with data-role="view" attribute set. Make sure that you instantiate the mobile application using the correct container.

Views represent the actual content that has to be displayed between the header and the footer that we defined while creating a layout. A layout cannot exist without a view and hence you see that error message in the console. To fix this error, you need to define a view for your mobile application.

5. Add the following to your `index.html` page:

```
<div data-role="view"
  data-layout="defaultLayout">
  Hello Kendo!!
</div>
```

As mentioned earlier, every widget needs to have a `role` data attribute to identify itself as a particular widget in the page. Here, the target element is defined as a `view` widget and tied to the layout by defining the `data-layout` attribute. The `data-layout` attribute has a value `defaultLayout` that is the same as the value for the `data-id` attribute of the layout that we defined earlier. This attaches the view to the layout and you will not see the error message anymore.

Similarly, you can have multiple Views defined in the page that can make use of the same layout (we will see this in the later part of this book). Now, there's only one pending task for the application to start working: initializing the application. A Kendo Mobile application can be initialized using the `Application` object. To do that, add the following code to the page:

```
<script>
  var app = new kendo.mobile.Application();
</script>
```

Include the previous script block right after references to jQuery and Kendo Mobile and before closing the body tag. This single line of JavaScript code will initialize your Kendo Mobile application and all the widgets with the `data-role` attribute.

The `Application` object is used for many other purposes and those will be covered in the upcoming recipes.

How it works...

When you run the `index.html` page in a browser, you will see a navbar and a tabstrip in the header and footer of the page. Also, the message **Hello Kendo!!** being shown in the body of the page. The following screenshot shows how it will look like when you view the page on an iPhone:

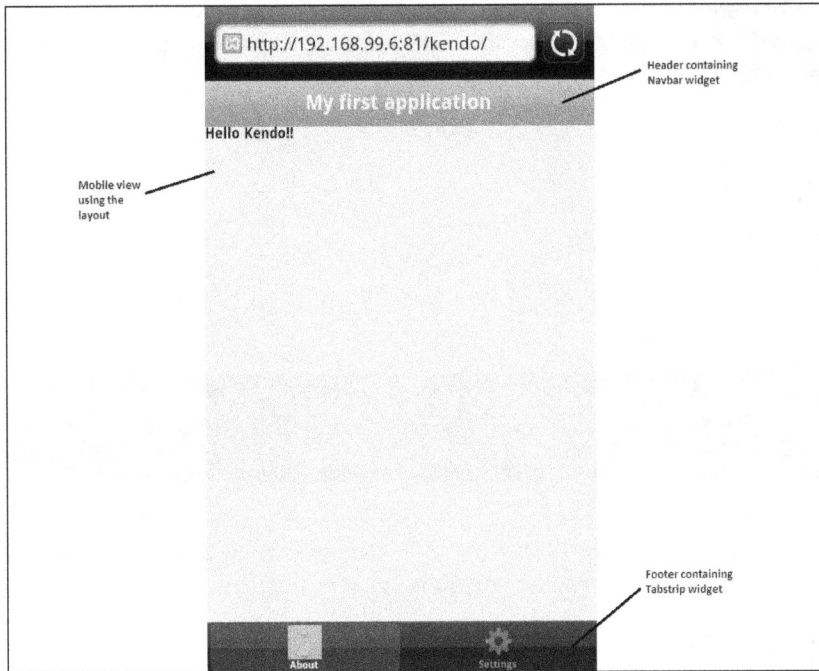

If you have noticed, this looks like a native iOS application. The framework has the capability to render the application that looks like a native application on a device. When you view the same page on an Android device, it will look like an native Android application, as shown in the following screenshot:

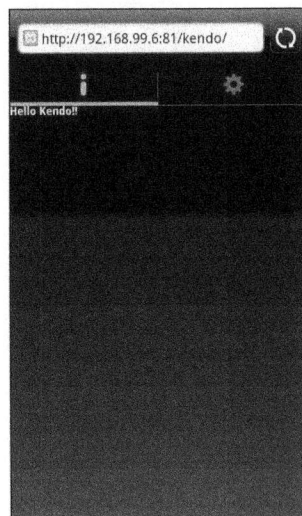

The framework identifies the platform on which the mobile application is being run and then provides native look and feel to the application. There are ways in which you can customize this behavior and this will be covered in the upcoming recipes.

In the next series of recipes, you will learn about the following core components of framework:

- Application
- Touch events
- Views
- Forms

Using the Application object to configure the application (Intermediate)

As seen in the earlier recipes, a Kendo Mobile application is initialized using the `kendo.mobile.Application` object. The `Application` object can also be used to provide initial configuration details and also in managing application navigation.

How to do it...

While initializing the mobile application, the `Application` object can be used to provide several configuration details. Perform the following steps:

1. The function `kendo.mobile.Application()` is called to initialize the application.
2. The first parameter to `kendo.mobile.Application()` is the target element, which is the container of various widgets with `data-role` attributes. Usually, it is the document's body tag, containing various widgets; hence, the default value for the first parameter is the reference to the `document.body` element.
3. The second parameter is an object that can be used to provide configuration details.

When you set the initial layout in a relatively larger application, you are likely to define multiple layouts and views. One of these layouts can be defined as an initial layout, which would then be rendered when the application loads. This configuration is provided while initializing the application using `kendo.mobile.Application()`.

The following code snippet defines two layouts – `defaultLayout` and `applicationLayout`. Also, it defines two views, `view1` and `view2`, as follows:

```
<div data-role="layout"
  data-id="defaultLayout">

  <header data-role="header">
```

```
    <div data-role="navbar">
        Default Layout Title
      </div>
    </header>

  </div>

  <div data-role="layout"
    data-id="applicationLayout">

    <header data-role="header">
      <div data-role="navbar">
        Application Layout Title
      </div>
    </header>

  </div>

  <div data-role="view"
    id="view1">
      Hello Kendo!!
  </div>

  <div data-role="view"
    id="view2">
      Hello Application!!
  </div>
```

In the previous code snippet, the views (`view1` and `view2`) do not specify any references to the layout widget that it likes to be associated with. Now, when you have two layouts in the page, the application would not be able to determine the layout to render when the application loads. This can be specified when the application is initialized using the `Application` object.

```
var app = new kendo.mobile.Application(document.body, {
  layout: "applicationLayout"
});
```

The `layout` key specifies the layout to be used when the application loads; here, `applicationLayout` is the value of the `data-id` attribute of the layout widget (`data-role="layout"`).

Similar to specifying an initial layout, you can also specify the initial view to render when the application loads. The first view in the page would be rendered by default, and if you would like to render any other view, specify the same while initializing the application as follows:

```
var app = new kendo.mobile.Application(document.body, {
  layout: "applicationLayout",
  initial: "view2"
});
```

Please note that here `view2` is the value of the `id` attribute that you want to render, while `applicationLayout` is the value of the `data-id` attribute.

How it works...

This screenshot shows how the application works:

When you execute the previous page, you will see that the view with the `id` attribute `view2` is shown on the layout with the `data-id` attribute `applicationLayout`.

There's more...

The `Application` object can also be used to provide other configuration details. For example, the `Application` object can be used to navigate to different views.

Navigating to different views

Consider an example where you have the following three views:

*   `index`
*   `loginview`
*   `signupview`

The `index` view has two buttons for **Login** and **Sign Up** as shown in the following code:

```
<div data-role="view"
  id="loginview">
  Login page
</div>
```

```
<div data-role="view"
  id="signupview">
  Sign Up page
</div>

<div data-role="view"
  id="index">

  <span class="button"
    data-role="button"
    id="login">
    In Login view
  </span>

  <span class="button"
    data-role="button"
    id="signup">
    In Sign Up view
  </span>

</div>
```

As explained earlier, you can set the initial view by specifying the same during application initialization.

```
var app = new kendo.mobile.Application(document.body, {
  initial: "index"
});
```

When the application loads, the `index` view will be shown, which contains two buttons: **Login** and **Sign Up**. On clicking on the **Login** button, you would like the application to navigate to `loginview`; similarly, on clicking on the **Signup** button, show `signupview`. To navigate to a different view, call `navigate` on the `Application` object as follows:

```
$('#login').on('click', function (event) {
  app.navigate('#loginview');
});

$('#signup').on('click', function (event) {
  app.navigate('#signupview');
});
```

The previous code snippet specifies a mouse-click event listener for all the **Login** and **Sign Up** buttons in the index view as shown in the following screenshot:

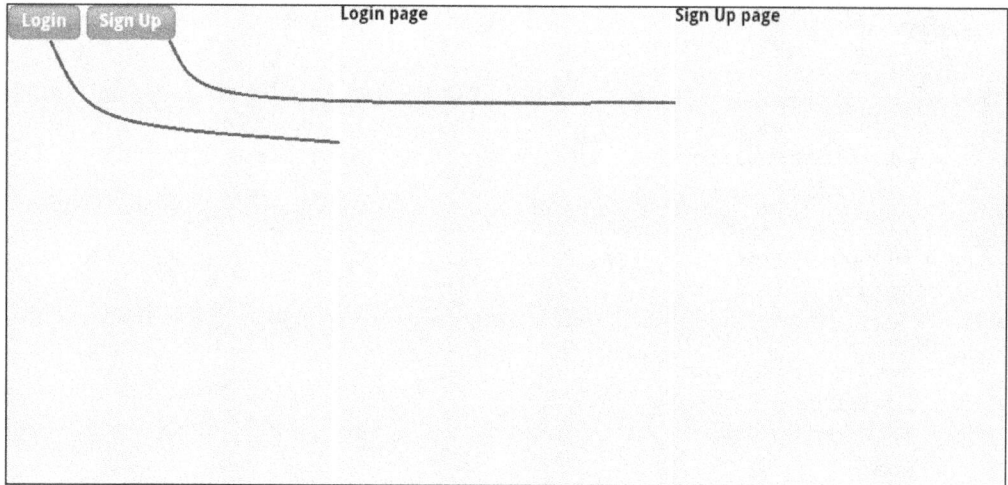

On clicking on the **Login** button, the `navigate` method is called on the `Application` object, specifying the view to navigate (`loginview`). This will then show the `login` view. Similarly, the `signup` view is shown when you click on the **Sign Up** button.

Adding touch events to your mobile application (Intermediate)

A user interacts with a mobile application using a touch-based interface. The mobile application should be able to provide quality support for touch-based user interfaces by interpreting finger activity on touch screens. The Kendo UI Mobile framework provides a set of APIs, using which the mobile application can handle user-initiated touch events, event sequences such as drags and swipes, and also in recognizing multi-touch gestures.

How to do it...

1. Create a document containing a layout or a view.
2. Define a widget with its `data-role` attribute set to `touch`.
3. Place this widget in the layout or the view created in step 1 as shown in the following code:

```
<div data-role="view"
    id="touchWidgetContainer">
```

```
<div id="touchSurface"
  data-role="touch"
  data-touchstart="touchstart"
  data-tap="tap">
  This is a touch surface.
    </div>

</div>
```

When the mobile application first runs, the touch widgets inside a view or a layout will be initialized. In the previous markup, you will notice that a widget with the `data-role` attribute `touch` is defined. It also defines a couple of other data attributes, `touchstart` and `tap`. These declare touch event handlers that need to be invoked when the user starts the touch (`touchstart`) and for handling user taps on the screen (`tap`).

The definition for the touch event handlers, `touchstart` and `tap`, are as shown in the following code:

```
function touchstart(event) {
  alert('Event - Touch Start' + " X= " + event.touch.x.location +
  " Y= " + event.touch.y.location);
}
function tap(event) {
  alert("Event - tap");
}.
```

The `touch` event object contains information on the active touch. It contains touch axis information; that is, the x and y coordinate where the touch was initiated. The properties `x.location` and `y.location` on the touch event object indicates the offset of the touch relative to the entire document. When a user touches the screen, the `touchstart` event is triggered. On the other hand, the `tap` event is fired when the user taps; that is, touches and then leaves the screen, similar to `mouseclick` and `mouseleave` on a desktop web application.

Apart from `touchstart` and `tap`, the framework can handle various other events such as `double tap`, `hold`, and `swipe`.

The following code snippet handles various touch events that have been mentioned previously:

```
<div data-role="view"
  id="touchWidgetContainer">

  <div id="touchSurface"
    data-role="touch"
    data-touchstart="touchstart"
    data-tap="tap"
    data-doubletap="doubletap"
    data-hold="hold"
```

```
        data-enable-swipe="true"
        data-swipe="swipe">
        Touch surface to handle various touch events<br>
        Touch, tap, double-tap, swipe and hold
    </div>

  </div>
```

Notice that there is another attribute, data-enable-swipe, that is set to true. By default, swipe events are not enabled; to enable them, you need to set the data-enable-swipe attribute to true. This will also disable the dragStart, drag, and dragEnd events that were to be triggered.

The corresponding event handlers are defined as follows:

```
<script>
  function touchstart(event) {
    alert('Event - Touch Start' + " X= "
    +event.touch.x.location + " Y= " + event.touch.y.location);
  }

  function tap(event) {
    alert('Event - Tap');
  }

  function doubletap(event) {
    alert('Event - Double tap');
  }

  function hold(event) {
    alert('Event - Hold');
  }

  function swipe(event)
  {
    alert('Swipe direction ' + event.direction);
  }
</script>
```

The previous code snippet defines event handlers for touchstart, tap, doubletap, hold, and swipe. Note that the swipe event handles horizontal swipes, and as observed in the previous code snippet, in the swipe event handler the touch event object includes the direction information indicating the direction in which the swipe was triggered. It can either be left or right.

How it works...

When you view the application on a mobile device and touch the screen, an alert popup, indicating the x and y location where the touch was initiated, would be shown as in the following screenshot:

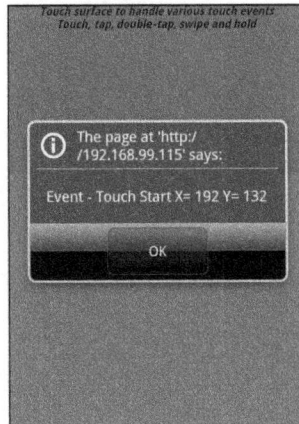

Displaying different types of views on a page (Intermediate)

As we have seen in the earlier recipes, a mobile application consists of a single HTML page with one or more mobile views in it. A Kendo Mobile View represents the screen in a Kendo Mobile application and it is a widget with the `data-role` attribute set to `view`. There are various types of views that can be added to the document, such as `listView`, `modalView`, `scrollView`, and others. The next few recipes focus on adding these views to the document.

How to do it...

1. A large application contains several views and specifying all of them in a single page would increase the size of the document.

2. Specify these views in separate pages (HTML pages) and specify the location of the HTML page in the `href` attribute of the anchor element.

3. The following is sample code that defines two buttons that are placed in the index page of the application:

```
<div data-role="view"
  data-title="Index View">

  <header data-role="header">
```

```
          <div data-role="navbar">
            <span data-role="view-title"></span>
          </div>

        </header>

        <div data-role="view">

          <a href="#localview"
            class="button"
            data-role="button">
            Local View
          </a>

          <a  href="./remoteview.html"
            class="button"
            data-role="button">
            Remote View
          </a>

        </div>

      </div>
```

How it works...

The previous code snippet defines an `Index` view, which includes a header containing a `Navbar` widget. Inside the `Navbar` widget, there is a `span` element with its `data-role` attribute set to `view-title`. This allows different views to define their choice of title to be shown in the `Navbar` widget. Notice that the container view defines the `data-title` attribute. The value of this attribute will be shown when the mobile application is initialized.

There are two buttons on the page, one to show a local view and another to show a remote view. Now let's define a widget that will be shown when you click on the `localview` button.

```
    <div data-role="view"
      id="localview"
      data-layout="mobile-view"
      data-title="Local view">
      From Local view
    </div>
```

The previous `div` element is added to the same document and it has an `id` attribute that is, `localview`. The previous `view` widget also specifies the `data-layout` attribute. Now let's define a layout for this view as follows:

```
    <div data-role="layout"
      data-id="mobile-view">
```

```
<header data-role="header">

<div data-role="navbar">
<a  class="nav-button"
   data-align="left"
   data-role="backbutton">

   Back
</a>

<span data-role="view-title"></span>
</div>

</header>

</div>
```

The previous layout defines the header with a Navbar and it is very similar to the view
that we defined earlier, except that this layout defines a widget backbutton
(data-role='backbutton'). This widget is used to navigate to the previous page
in the browser's history.

Now, when you tap on the **Local view** button, you will see that the application is navigated to
the local view, the Navbar shows the title as **Local view**, and the body of the page will show
the text **From local view**. Also, on tapping the **back** button defined in the header, you will be
taken to the index page. We have already defined an anchor element in the document with
it's href attribute set to remoteview.html. Now let's create a new page, remoteview.
html, and define a view in it as follows:

```
<div data-role="view"
   data-layout="mobile-view"
   data-title="Remote view">

   This page is from Remote view
</div>
```

This widget is similar to the widget that we defined while creating a local view, except that it
is defined in a different document, that is, remoteview.html. Also notice that it makes a
reference to the layout widget that we defined in the index document. Now, when you tap on
the remote view button, the view defined in the remoteview.html page will be shown.

> Please note that the CSS and JavaScript files required for the remote
> document (remoteview.html) should be specified in the index
> document. This is because these files will not be evaluated when they
> are specified in the remote document.

When you tap on the **Local view** button, the view defined in the same document is shown;
when you tap on the **Remote View** button, the view defined in remote.html is shown.

There's more...

Here we will see how you can define transition effects while navigating from one view to the other.

Specifying view transitions

While transitioning from one view to the other, you can specify the transition effect that needs to be applied, using the `data-transition` attribute. The following values can be set as value to the data-transition attribute:

- ▶ **slide**: This transition effect slides the old view content to the left and the new view content slides in its place. You can specify the direction using the slide (direction). By default, the direction is left; the other option is right.

- ▶ **zoom**: Here, the new view content zooms from the center of the old view. The old view content will fade out and the new view content will be shown.

- ▶ **fade**: The new content fades in on top of the old view. The old view content will fade out, showing the content from the new view.

- ▶ **overlay**: The overlay effect is similar to the slide effect, except that the previous view remains under the new one. The transition direction can be specified using overlay (direction). By default, the direction is left; other supported directions include right, up, and down.

In all of the transition effects mentioned, the content along with its header and footer are shown.

It is also possible to specify the transition effect for the entire application instead of specifying the `data-transition` attribute for each view widget in the document. When initializing the application using the `Application` object, specify the `transition` property with the desired effect as its value.

```
var app = new kendo.mobile.Application(document.body, {
  transition: "zoom"
});
```

This allows the transition effect to be applied to the entire application.

Adding form elements to a mobile page (Simple)

Most mobile applications require data to be captured from the user input fields and they make use of forms. The Kendo UI Mobile framework allows you to add form elements to the page and provides styling for various platforms.

How to do it...

The mobile framework supports the adding of various types of input elements to the form such as text, password, e-mail, number, telephone, search, URL, date, time, month, and date time.

1. Create an HTML document containing a form element.

2. Add input fields of type `text`, `password`, `email`, `date`, and `radio`. The following is a sample markup that shows a form on a page:

```html
<div id="forms"
  data-role="view"
  data-title="Form Elements"
  data-layout="mobile-view">

<form action="./index.html">

<ul data-role="listview" data-style="inset">

  <li>
    <label>Full Name</label>
    <input type="text" placeholder="Full Name"/>
  </li>

  <li>
    <label>Password</label>
    <input
      type="password"
    placeholder="Password" />
  </li>

  <li>
    <label>Email</label>
    <input
      type="email"
    placeholder="username@domain.com" />
  </li>

  <li>
    <label>Date of Birth</label>
    <input type="date" />
  </li>

  <li>
    <label>Education</label>
    <select>
      <option value="Bachelors">
```

```
            Bachelors
          </option>
          <option value="Masters">
            Masters
          </option>
          <option value="Postgraduation">
            Post Graduation
          </option>
        </select>
      </li>

  </ul>

  <ul data-role="listview"
    data-style="inset" data-type="group">
    <li>Gender
    <ul>
    <li>
      <label>
        <input name="units" type="radio" checked="checked" />
      MALE</label>
    </li>
    <li>
      <label>
        <input name="units" type="radio" />
      FEMALE</label>
      </li>
    </ul>
    </li>
    <li>
      <button type="submit" data-
role="button">Submit</button>
    </li>
    </ul>
  </form>
</div>
```

How it works...

As seen in the previous markup, the form elements are added to the document, and when you run the same on a mobile device, the following output is shown:

If you have noticed the code snippet, we have made use of a new widget, `ListView`. The `ListView` widget is generally used when you have a list of elements to be shown on the page.

Next, you will learn about the various widgets that are available for use in building a Kendo mobile application.

Creating a list using the ListView widget (Intermediate)

The Kendo Mobile `ListView` widget allows you to display a list of items on the page. The list can be flat or grouped. We have already seen an example of the `ListView` widget in the previous recipe. A `ListView` widget can be created by assigning the value `listview` to the `data-role` attribute of an ordered or unordered list. The list values can be specified in the markup or bound to a `DataSource` instance.

How to do it...

Let's add a `ListView` widget containing detail buttons to the page. A detail button allows you to specify an action button for each list item (each row) in the list.

1. To create a `ListView` widget, create an unordered list and set the `data-role` attribute to `listview`.

2. Add detail buttons by adding anchor elements with the `data-role` attribute set to `detailbutton`. The following is the sample code:

```
<div data-role="view">
  <ul data-role="listview"
  data-style="inset"
  data-type="group">

    <li>Default Buttons
      <ul>
        <li>
          <a>Add </a>
          <a data-role="detailbutton"
            data-style="contactadd">
          </a>
        </li>
        <li>
          <a>Close </a>
          <a data-role="detailbutton"
            data-style="detaildisclose">
          </a>
        </li>
        <li>
          <a>Insert </a>
          <a data-role="detailbutton"
            data-style="rowinsert">
          </a>
        </li>
        <li>
          <a>Delete </a>
            <a data-role="detailbutton"
              data-style="rowdelete">
            </a>
        </li>
      </ul>
    </li>

  </ul>
</div>
```

The previous code snippet creates a `ListView` widget and specifies detail buttons for each item in the list.

How it works...

When you run the previous page, you will see a list of items with detail buttons aligned to the right of the list item.

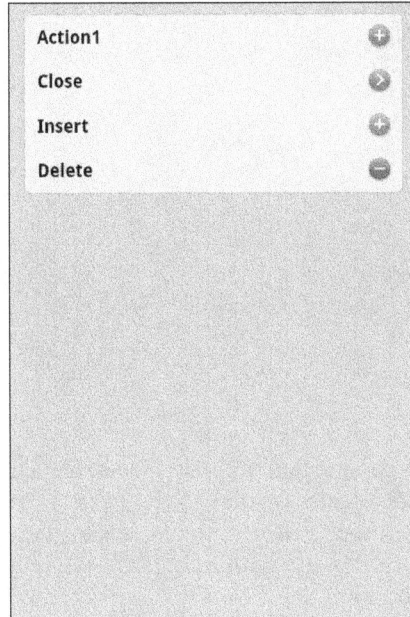

The `data-styles` attribute of a **Detail** button can contain one of these values: `contactadd`, `detaildisclose`, `rowinsert`, and `rowdelete`. Apart from specifying the `data-style` attribute for a `detailbutton` widget, you can specify custom icons through the `data-icon` attribute:

```
<li>
  <a>Favorites </a>
  <a data-role="detailbutton"
  data-icon="favorites">
  </a>
</li>
```

The list item mentioned previously does not include the `data-style` attribute; instead, a `data-icon` attribute is defined. Now, when you run the page, you will see the `favorites` icon shown for the list item as shown in the following screenshot:

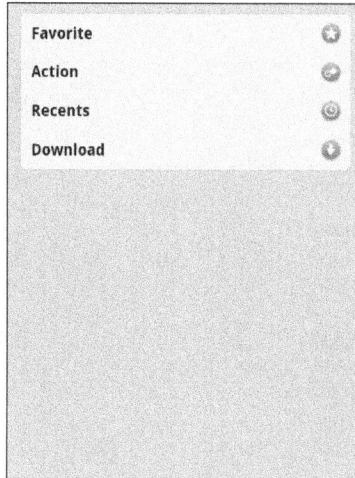

The `data-icon` attribute can contain one of these values: `about`, `action`, `add`, `bookmarks`, `camera`, `cart`, `compose`, `contacts`, `details`, `downloads`, `fastforward`, `favorites`, `featured`, `toprated`, `globe`, `history`, `home`, `info`, `more`, `mostrecent`, `mostviewed`, `organize`, `pause`, `play`, `recents`, `refresh`, `reply`, `rewind`, `search`, `settings`, `share`, `stop`, and `trash`.

The mentioned icons would suffice for most of the applications. However, you can include your own icon by defining a CSS class and specifying the `data-icon` value as custom. This will look for the class definition, `km-class`, in your CSS stylesheet.

There's more...

In the previous recipe, we have created `ListView` using an unordered list and specified a list of items in the markup. It is also possible to create a `ListView` widget that is populated from a `DataSource` widget.

Binding a mobile ListView to a DataSource widget

The mobile `ListView` widget can be bound to a JavaScript array and the mobile framework allows you to specify the `DataSource` for the `ListView` widgets:

```
<div data-role="view"
  data-init="flatlistviewinit">

  <ul id="flatlistview"></ul>

</div>
```

The previous markup does not contain any list items. It specifies the container's `ul` element, which will contain the list of items from the `DataSource`. Note that the view contains the `data-init` attribute. This attribute specifies the JavaScript callback function to invoke when the framework is initializing the widgets in the document.

The function `flatlistviewinit` is used to bind the `DataSource` to the unordered list in the markup.

```
var flatData = ["Australia", "Barbados", "Canada", "Denmark",
"Egypt", "Finland", "Germany", "Hungary", "India", "Japan"];

function flatlistviewinit(){

  $('#flatlistview').kendoMobileListView({
    dataSource: flatData
  });

}
```

The previous code snippet defines an array containing a list of country names. The function `flatlistviewinit` is invoked by the framework when it tries to initialize the view in the document. This function binds the array to the `ul` element defined in the markup. The function `kendoMobileListView` is called on the specified selector to initialize it as a `ListView` widget. The function also specifies the `datasource` value to be used for the `ListView` widget. In this case, the `DataSource` widget is the array containing the list of country names.

When you execute this page, you will see that a list view is created, which displays a list of countries that we specified in the array.

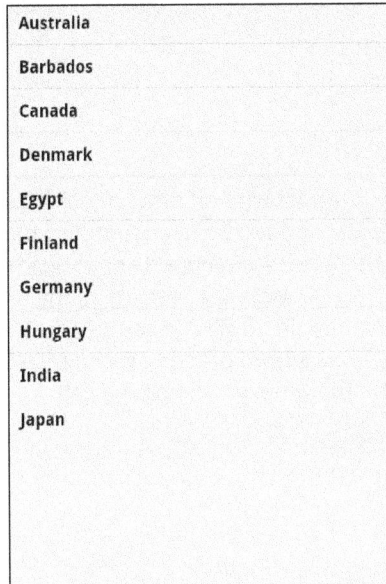

| Australia |
| Barbados |
| Canada |
| Denmark |
| Egypt |
| Finland |
| Germany |
| Hungary |
| India |
| Japan |

Grouping in a ListView widget

In the previous example, we listed countries; in this section, we will group these countries based on the continent in which they belong.

To group each of these countries, let's create an array of JavaScript objects. Each object in the array will contain the country name and the continent to which it belongs.

```
var groupedData = [
    {name: "Ghana", continent: "Africa"},
    {name: "India", continent: "Asia"},
    {name: "Australia", continent: "Oceania"},
    {name: "France", continent: "Europe"},
    {name: "Mexico", continent: "N. AMERICA"},
    {name: "Sri Lanka", continent: "Asia"},
    {name: "Argentina", continent: "S. AMERICA"},
    {name: "Kenya", continent: "Africa"},
    {name: "Italy", continent: "Europe"},
    {name: "United States", continent: "N. AMERICA"},
    {name: "New Zealand", continent: "Oceania"},
    {name: "Brazil", continent: "S. AMERICA"},
];
```

Now let's create a function that will initialize the `ListView` widget with the previous array.

```
function groupedlistviewinit() {
  $('#groupedlistview').kendoMobileListView({
    dataSource: kendo.data.DataSource.create({
      data: groupedData, group: "continent"
    }),
    template: '${name}',
    fixedHeaders: true
  });
}
```

Here we are initializing an unordered list with an array of objects. While initializing the widget, we are specifying the `datasource` value to be used and also the property by which the list items should be grouped. The `template` property specifies the template to use when adding list elements to the `ListView` widget. The value of the template property in this case is `${name}`. When the application is run, it will replace `${name}` with the name property specified in the object. The `fixedHeaders` property contains a Boolean true as its value; this makes the headers fix to the top when you scroll the list.

When you run this page, you will see a list of items shown on the page and these are grouped by the continent names.

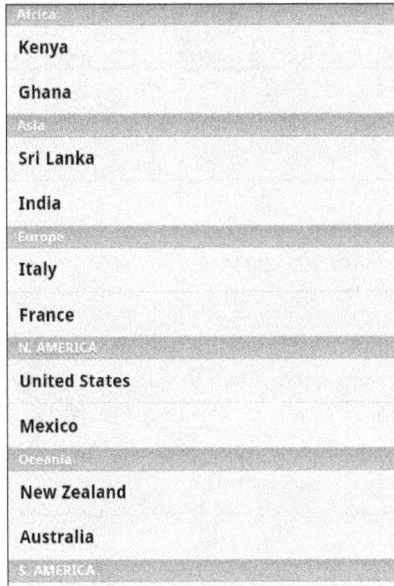

Africa
Kenya
Ghana
Asia
Sri Lanka
India
Europe
Italy
France
N. AMERICA
United States
Mexico
Oceania
New Zealand
Australia
S. AMERICA

When you scroll, you will see that the headers containing the continent name fix to the top, as shown in the following screenshot:

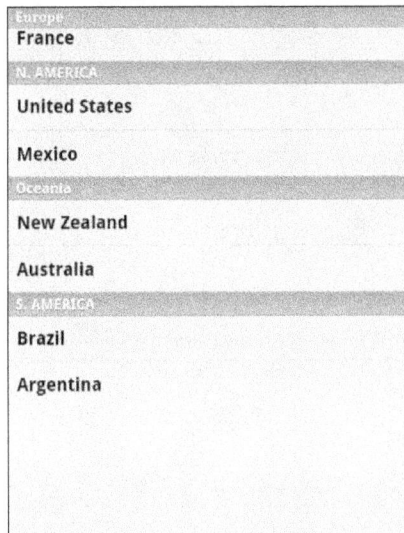

Europe
France
N. AMERICA
United States
Mexico
Oceania
New Zealand
Australia
S. AMERICA
Brazil
Argentina

The header will change only when a new group containing a list of country names is shown at the top of the list.

Showing a list of actions to perform using the ActionSheet widget (Advanced)

The Kendo Mobile `ActionSheet` widget is used to show a list of actions to perform when a user taps on an element on the screen. The `ActionSheet` widget slides from the bottom and shows a list of actions to perform against the tapped element on the screen.

How to do it...

1. Create a `ListView` widget with each list item containing an anchor element with its `data-rel` attribute set to `actionsheet`.

2. Create an `ActionSheet` widget by setting the `data-role` attribute to `actionsheet`.

3. The `href` attribute of the anchor elements in the `ListView` widget should be the same as the `id` attribute of the `actionsheet` widget.

```
<div data-role="view">
  <ul data-role="listview"
    data-style="inset"
    data-type="group">

    <li>
      <ul>
        <li>
          <a data-rel="actionsheet"
            href="#optionActionSheet">
            Action 1
          </a>
        </li>
        <li>
          <a data-rel="actionsheet"
            href="#optionActionSheet">
            Action 2
          </a>
        </li>
        <li>
          <a data-rel="actionsheet"
            href="#optionActionSheet">
            Action 3
          </a>
        </li>
      </ul>
    </li>

  </ul>

  <ul data-role="actionsheet" id="optionActionSheet">
```

```
        <li><a data-action="option1">Option 1</a></li>
        <li><a data-action="option2">Option 2</a></li>
        <li><a data-action="option3">Option 3</a></li>
      </ul>
    </div>
```

The previous code snippet defines a view containing a `ListView` widget. The `ListView` widget contains anchor elements of the following form:

```
<a data-rel="actionsheet"
   href="#optionActionSheet">
   Action 1
</a>
```

Here, the anchor element specifies the `data-rel` attribute with its value as `actionsheet`. This `data-rel` attribute is used to open the `ActionSheet` widget from any navigational widget such as a button, an anchor link item, or a tabstrip. Also, the `href` attribute of the anchor element specifies the `id` value of the `ActionSheet` widget (`openActionSheet`) to be invoked.

The `ActionSheet` widget is defined with the `data-role` attribute set to `actionsheet` and its `id` attribute set to `openActionSheet`. This widget contains three list items containing a list of actions to perform. The `data-action` attribute is used to specify the JavaScript function to invoke when the user taps one of the options.

How it works...

When you execute the previous code snippet, you will see that a `ListView` widget is shown as follows:

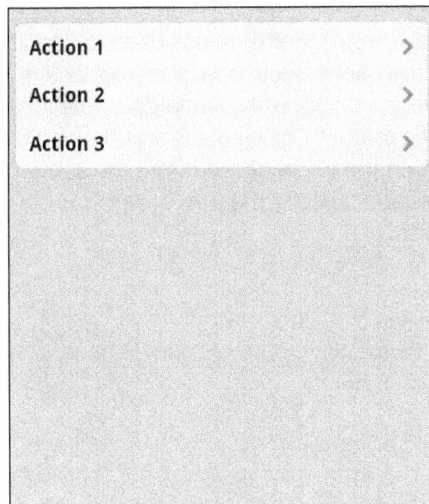

On clicking on any of the list items in the `ListView` widget, the `ActionSheet` widget will slide in from the bottom of the screen to show a list of options, as shown in the following screenshot:

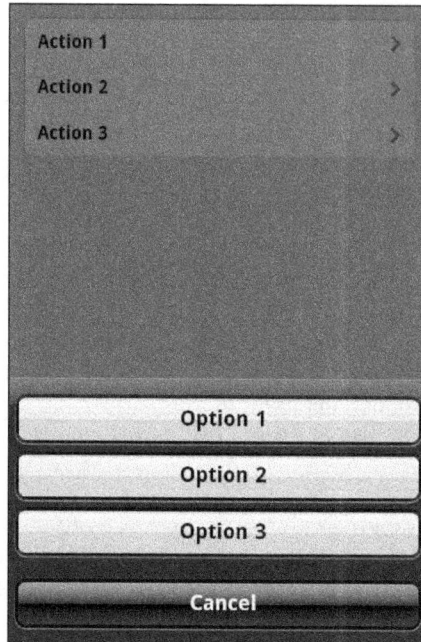

Notice that along with the three options, another option with the value **Cancel** is also added to the list. This allows the user to cancel the task and hide the `ActionSheet` widget.

There's more...

As mentioned earlier, the `data-action` attribute is used to specify the JavaScript callback function to be invoked when the user selects one of the options in the `ActionSheet` widget. This callback function receives an object with two fields, namely, target and context. The target field holds the reference to the DOM element that opened the `ActionSheet` widget and the context field will contain the value passed from the same DOM element. To pass a value to the `ActionSheet` widget, specify the `data-actionsheet-context` attribute with the value that you need to pass.

```
<a id="firstItem"
  data-rel="actionsheet"
  data-actionsheet-context="1"
  href="#optionActionSheet">
  Action 1
</a>
```

In the previous markup, one of the list items is updated to contain a `data-actionsheet-context` attribute with the value `1`. The JavaScript function is defined as follows:

```
function option1 (e) {
  console.log(e.target); // $('#firstItem')
  console.log(e.context); // 1
}
```

Here, the target field will refer to the DOM element that invoked the `ActionSheet` widget and the context field will contain the value 1, which was passed from the DOM element that invoked the `ActionSheet` widget.

Displaying a Modal window using the ModalView widget (Advanced)

A `ModalView` widget is similar to an `ActionSheet` widget, which is invoked by tapping on one of the widgets on the screen. A `ModalView` widget is used to present a window-like view as an overlay over an existing view in the page. In case of `ActionSheet`, the widget will slide up from the bottom of the screen, whereas a `ModalView` widget will be shown at the center of the screen.

How to do it...

1. Create an anchor element with its `data-rel` attribute set to `modalview`.
2. Create a `ModalView` widget by setting the `data-role` attribute to `modalview`.
3. The anchor element's `href` attribute should be same as the modal view's `id` attribute, as shown in the following code:

```
<div data-role="view">
  <a data-role="button"
     data-rel="modalview"
     href="#modalview-form">

     Login
  </a>
</div>

<div data-role="modalview"
  id="modalview-form"
  style="width: 70%; height: 270px;">

  <div data-role="header">
    <div data-role="navbar">

      <span>Login</span>
```

```
        <a data-click="closeBtnHandler"
          data-role="button"
          data-align="right">

          Cancel
        </a>

      </div>
    </div>

    <ul data-role="listview"
      data-style="inset">

      <li>
        <label for="username">Username:</label>
        <input type="text" id="username" />
      </li>
      <li>
        <label for="password">Password:</label>
        <input type="password" id="password" />
      </li>

    </ul>

    <a data-click="loginBtnHandler"
      type="button"
      data-role="button"
      style="margin-left: 40%;">

      Login
    </a>
    <a data-click="registerBtnHandler"
      type="button"
      data-role="button">

      Register
    </a>
  </div>
```

The previous code is very similar to the `ActionSheet` widget that we created in the last recipe. Here, the view specifies the value of the `data-rel` attribute as `modalview` and also specifies the `id` value of the `ModalView` widget (that is, `modalview-form`) as it's `href` attribute.

The `ModalView` widget has the `id` attribute set to `modalview-form` and the `data-role` attribute set to `modalview` to mark the target element as a `ModalView` widget. The widget can then contain any number of elements in it. The following widgets are added to the previous code snippet: a header containing the Navbar with the **Cancel** button, form elements that would capture the user's login credentials, and buttons to handle the login and register functionality.

How it works...

When the page loads, you will see a **Login** button shown. On clicking on the **Login** button, a modal view containing the form elements is shown.

There's more...

For a `ModalView` widget, you can specify the `data-open` attribute whose value will be the name of a JavaScript callback function. This function is invoked whenever the `ModalView` widget is opened.

```
<div
   data-role="modalview"
   id="modalview-form"
   data-open="openModalView">

   ....
</div>
```

This is particularly helpful when you are managing the state of the application. For example, you may want to execute a JavaScript function that changes the state of the application when the `ModalView` widget is opened.

Creating a TabStrip widget for a mobile application (Intermediate)

A `TabStrip` widget is used to display a group of navigation buttons. More often than not, these navigation buttons are placed in the footer of the application's layout widget.

How to do it...

The `TabStrip` widget is created by assigning the value `tabstrip` to the `data-role` attribute of the target element. Each tab or button in the `TabStrip` widget is used to show one of the views defined in the application. On clicking the tab, the current view as well as the selected tab's state is updated.

1. Create a document containing a layout widget with a navbar in the header.
2. Create a `TabStrip` widget by setting the `data-role` attribute to `tabstrip`.
3. Place the `Tabstrip` widget in the footer of the layout widget.

```
<div data-role="layout"
  data-id="applayout">

  <div data-role="header">
    <div data-role="navbar">
      <span data-role="view-title"></span>
    </div>
  </div>

  <div data-role="footer">
    <div data-role="tabstrip">
      <a href="#contactslist"
        data-icon="contacts">
        Contacts
      </a>
      <a href="#favorites"
        data-icon="favorites">
        Favorites
      </a>
      <a href="#about"
        data-icon="about">
        About
      </a>
    </div>
  </div>

</div>
```

The previous code snippet defines an application-wide layout widget and it has the header and footer widgets defined in it. The footer widget has the `TabStrip` widget (`data-role='tabstrip'`). The `TabStrip` widget has three anchor elements and each of these anchor elements have an `href` and `data-icon` attribute. The `href` attribute refers to the view that should be displayed when the user selects the tab. The `data-icon` attribute specifies the icon to use for the tab. The framework provides several icons that can be used while defining tabs in the `TabStrip` widget. You can also add your own set of icons by defining the respective CSS class in the stylesheet.

Now let's add the three views that are mentioned in the `TabStrip` widget.

```
<div data-role="view"
   id="contactslist"
   data-layout="applayout"
   data-title="Contacts">

  <ul data-role="listview"
     data-style="inset"
     data-type="group">

    <li>
      <ul>
        <li>Adam</li>
        <li>Ben</li>
        <li>Charlie</li>
        <li>David</li>
        <li>Earl</li>
        <li>Frank</li>
        <li>Greg</li>
        <li>Hamish</li>
        <li>Jack</li>
        <li>Mellisa</li>
        <li>Terry</li>
        <li>Victoria</li>
      </ul>
    </li>

  </ul>

</div>
<div data-role="view"
   id="favorites"
   data-layout="applayout"
   data-title="Favorites">

  <ul data-role="listview"
     data-style="inset"
     data-type="group">

    <li>
      <ul>
        <li>Ben</li>
```

```
            <li>Charlie</li>
            <li>David</li>
            <li>Frank</li>
            <li>Terry</li>
            <li>Victoria</li>
          </ul>
        </li>
      </ul>
    </div>

    <div data-role="view"
       id="about"
       data-layout="applayout"
       data-title="About">

       A simple Tabstrip application

    </div>
```

The previous code snippet defines three views. Notice that the `id` attribute of each of these views is specified as `href` for the anchor elements defined in `TabStrip`.

How it works...

When you load the previous page, you will see that a list of contacts (the `contactslist` view) is shown and the first tab in the `TabStrip` widget is selected, as shown in the following screenshot:

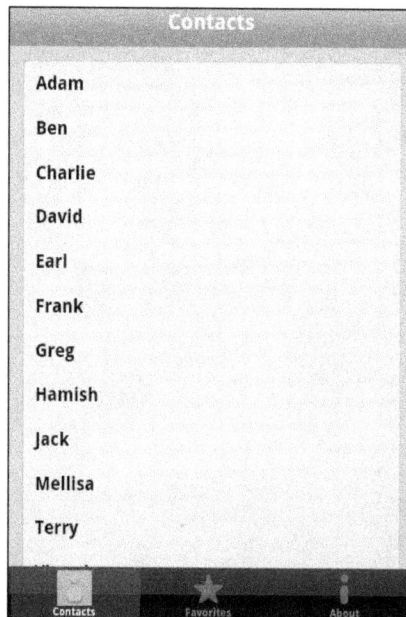

When you select the **Favorites** tab (`<a href=#favorites>Favorites</a>`), the selected tab and the view is updated to show a list of contacts marked as **Favorites**, as shown in the following screenshot:

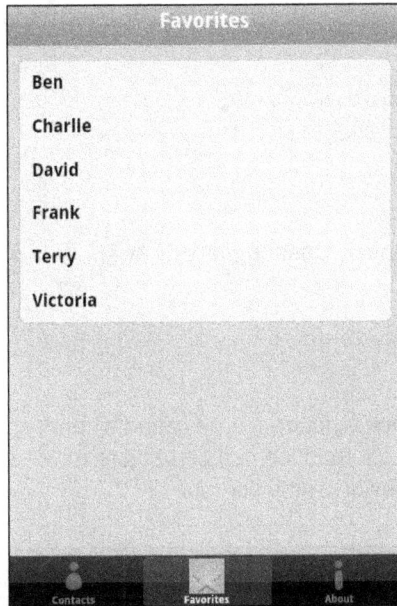

Again, when you select the **About** tab, the **About** view is shown.

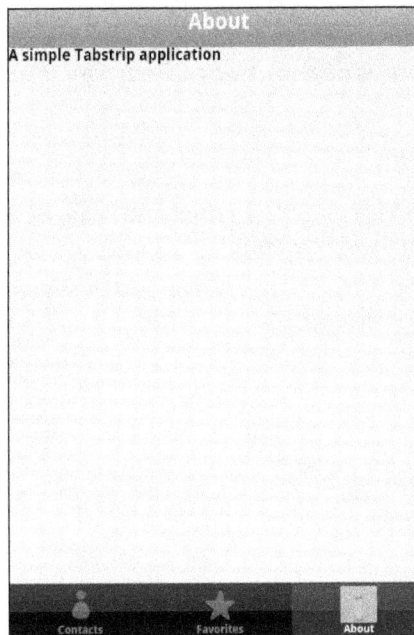

There's more...

You can define a JavaScript callback function that is fired when you select a tab in the `TabStrip` widget. To do that, specify the `data-select` attribute for the `Tabstrip` widget as follows:

```
<div data-role="tabstrip"
  data-select="selectEvent">
  ....
</div>
```

Now define the JavaScript callback function `selectEvent`.

```
function selectEvent () {
  console.log('Select Event');
}
```

The previous JavaScript callback function will be called whenever the user selects the tab in the `TabStrip` widget. A callback function can be used to make a call to the analytics server, which will record the user behavior on the screen.

Using the ScrollView widget to navigate through the application (Intermediate)

A `ScrollView` widget is used in Picture-Gallery-like applications, where you would like to scroll to the next page to see the next picture in the gallery. The widget allows you to move to the next page or to the previous page by swiping from right to left or left to right.

How to do it...

1. A `ScrollView` widget is created by setting the value `scrollview` to the `data-role` attribute on the target element.
2. Each widget inside the `ScrollView` widget is defined as a `page` widget by setting the `data-role` attribute to `page`.

Let's use the `ScrollView` widget to create a photo gallery application. This application will show one image at a time, and on swiping from right to left or vice versa, the image defined in the next or the previous page will be shown.

```
<div data-role="view"
  id="scrollviewContainer">

  <div data-role="scrollview">

    <div data-role="page">
      <img src="images/image1.jpg"/>
    </div><div data-role="page">
      <img src="images/image2.jpg"/>
    </div><div data-role="page">
      <img src="images/image3.jpg"/>
    </div><div data-role="page">
      <img src="images/image4.jpg"/>
    </div><div data-role="page">
      <img src="images/image5.jpg"/>
    </div><div data-role="page">
      <img src="images/image6.jpg"/>
    </div><div data-role="page">
      <img src="images/image7.jpg"/>
    </div>

  </div>

</div>
```

The previous code snippet defines a view that contains the `ScrollView` widget. The `ScrollView` widget contains seven `page` widgets (`data-role='page'`), each of which has an `image` tag specified in it.

> Notice that the markup contains no whitespaces between the `page` widgets. This is intentional, because when an extra space is specified, an additional page is added to the view.

How it works...

When the page loads, it initializes the `ScrollView` widget and displays the first image in the set. It also displays seven buttons corresponding to the seven images on the screen. By default, the first button in the set is selected since the first page is shown when the application is viewed.

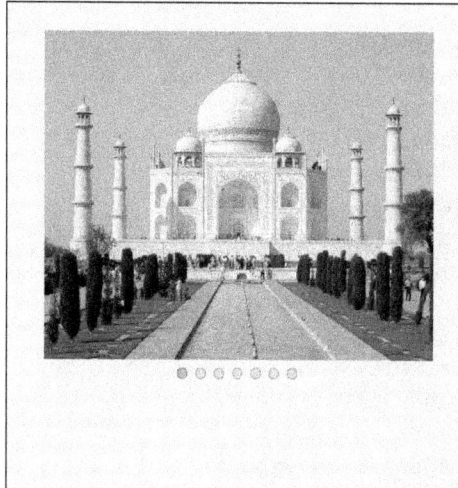

On swiping from right to left, the next page containing the image is shown. This will also update the selected button in the `ScrollView` widget, as shown in the following screenshot:

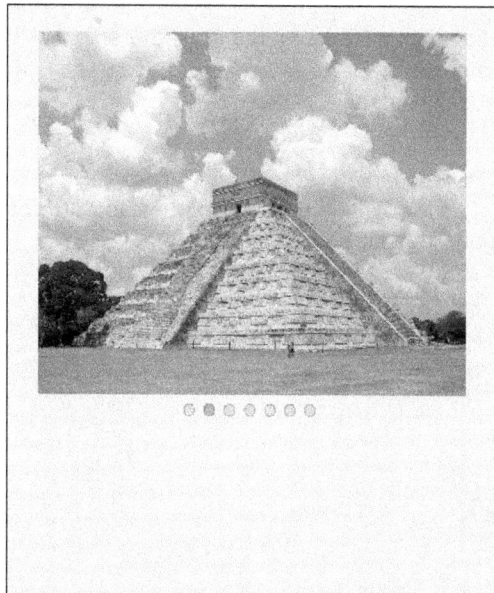

There's more...

You can also specify a JavaScript callback function when the page widget has changed. To do that, define the `data-change` attribute on the `ScrollView` widget.

```
<div data-role="scrollview"
  data-change="pageChange">
  ......
</div>
```

The JavaScript callback function would be as follows:

```
function pageChange() {
  console.log('New Page');
}
```

The `pageChange` function is executed when you swipe on the device to see the next page.

Here we will see how an application created with Kendo UI Mobile is rendered on different platforms, namely iOS, Android, and Blackberry. Also, how the framework handles different orientations, portrait and landscape.

Rendering with native look and feel using adaptive rendering technique (Simple)

Today, developers are challenged to build applications that are not only rich in functionality but also render on different devices with native look and feel. Maintaining a different code base for different devices can slow down the developer productivity and will require more time and effort to get the right output.

The Kendo UI Mobile framework is designed to solve the mentioned problems. It allows developers to build great experiences for the mobile applications using HTML5 and JavaScript. The framework itself takes care of rendering the application on different devices and provides native look and feel on different platforms. This allows developers to focus on building the functionality and letting the framework handle the differences between different platforms.

In most of the recipes mentioned in the book, you would have seen the output that resembles the native look and feel of an iOS device. When you view the same application on an Android or Blackberry device, you will see that the application renders differently on these devices. The framework takes care of rendering the application on different mobile platforms in a way that gives a native look and feel to your application. The framework supports adaptive rendering on iOS, Android, and Blackberry platforms.

How to do it...

1. Let's take a look at the applications we have built in the previous recipes and see how they render on different devices. Applications containing `Navbar` and `TabStrip` will be displayed as shown in the following screenshot:

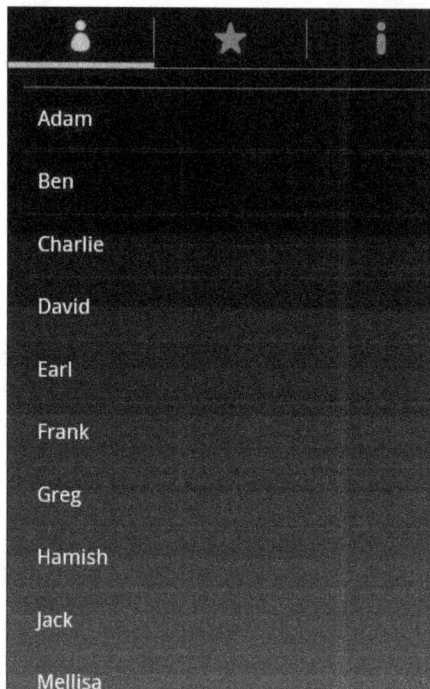

2. Notice how the application changes the layout on the Android device to show the `TabStrip` widget at the top and also the look and feel of the `ListView` widget. Another thing to notice here is that `Navbar` is not visible on the Android device. To force the application to the show the `Navbar` widget on an Android device, you can add the following CSS code snippet:

```
.km-android .km-navbar .km-view-title
{
  visibility: visible;
}
```

This forces the application to the show Navbar and it is rendered at the bottom of the screen:

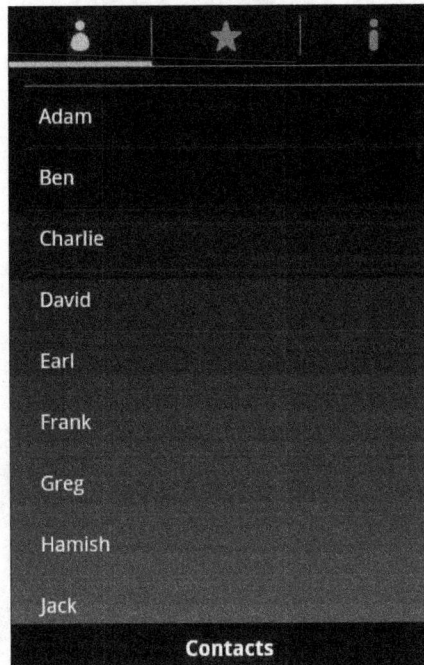

The adaptive rendering capability of the Kendo Mobile framework certainly allows you to build applications rapidly without being concerned about its rendering on different platforms. However, in some scenarios, you would like to render the same look and feel across all platforms. For example, you would like the iOS look and feel to be applied across all platforms. The framework can be configured to force the look and feel of a particular platform. To do that, specify the `platform` property with the platform name as its value when initializing the application.

```
var app = new kendo.mobile.Application(document.body, {
  platform: "ios"
});
```

The previous code snippet will force the application to render the iOS look and feel on all platforms.

Handling change in the layout orientation using the automatic layout system (Simple)

Another functionality that the framework provides is in handling of the change in the layout orientation. The framework re-renders the application when the layout's orientation is changed from portrait to landscape and vice versa.

How to do it...

1. Take a look at the same application containing the `Navbar`, a `TabStrip` widget, and a list of elements in `ListView`.

2. When you change the orientation of the device, the framework's layout engine will automatically position elements as shown in the following screenshot:

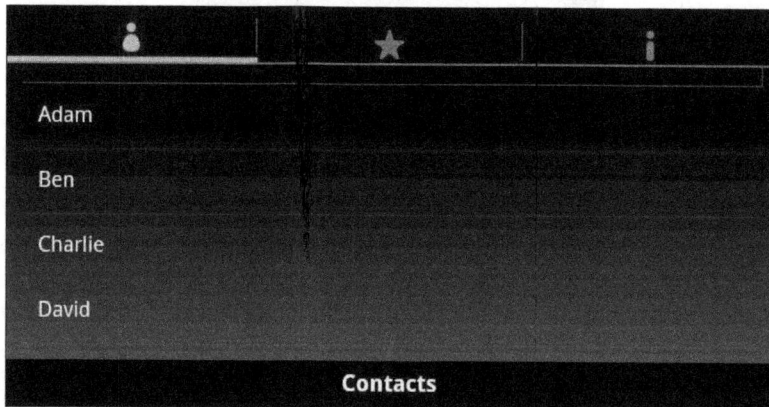

As shown in the previous screenshot, the layout changes to adapt to the new orientation.

[PACKT] Thank you for buying
PUBLISHING **Instant Kendo UI Mobile**

About Packt Publishing

Packt, pronounced 'packed', published its first book "*Mastering phpMyAdmin for Effective MySQL Management*" in April 2004 and subsequently continued to specialize in publishing highly focused books on specific technologies and solutions.

Our books and publications share the experiences of your fellow IT professionals in adapting and customizing today's systems, applications, and frameworks. Our solution based books give you the knowledge and power to customize the software and technologies you're using to get the job done. Packt books are more specific and less general than the IT books you have seen in the past. Our unique business model allows us to bring you more focused information, giving you more of what you need to know, and less of what you don't.

Packt is a modern, yet unique publishing company, which focuses on producing quality, cutting-edge books for communities of developers, administrators, and newbies alike. For more information, please visit our website: www.packtpub.com.

Writing for Packt

We welcome all inquiries from people who are interested in authoring. Book proposals should be sent to author@packtpub.com. If your book idea is still at an early stage and you would like to discuss it first before writing a formal book proposal, contact us; one of our commissioning editors will get in touch with you.

We're not just looking for published authors; if you have strong technical skills but no writing experience, our experienced editors can help you develop a writing career, or simply get some additional reward for your expertise.

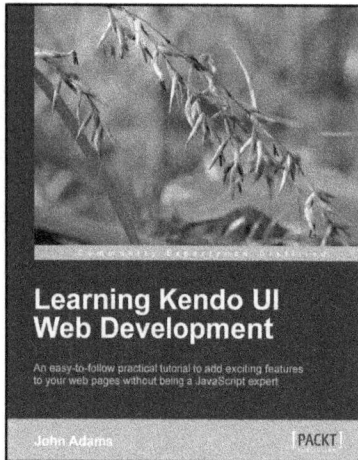

Learning Kendo UI Web Development

ISBN: 978-1-84969-434-6   Paperback: 288 pages

An easy-to-follow practical tutorial to add exciting features to your web pages without being a JavaScript expert

1. Learn from clear and specific examples on how to utilize the full range of the Kendo UI tool set for the web

2. Add powerful tools to your website supported by a familiar and trusted name in innovative technology

3. Learn how to add amazing features with clear examples and make your website more interactive without being a JavaScript expert

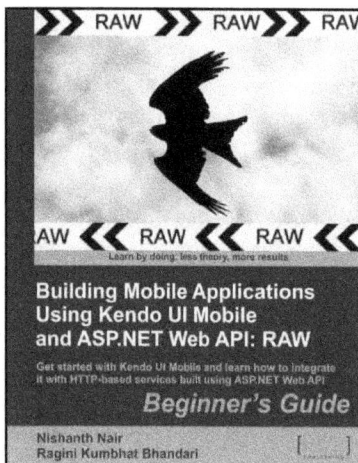

Building Mobile Applications with Kendo UI Mobile: RAW

ISBN: 978-1-78216-092-2   Paperback: 300 pages

Get started with Kendo UI Mobile and learn how to integrate it with HTTP-based services built using ASP.NET Web API

1. Learn the basics of developing mobile applications using HTML5 and create an end-to-end mobile application from scratch

2. Discover all about Kendo UI Mobile, ASP .NET Web API, and how to integrate them

3. Understand how to organize your JavaScript code to achieve extensibility and maintainability

4. Get your hands dirty in a jiffy with 50+ jsFiddle examples

Please check **www.PacktPub.com** for information on our titles

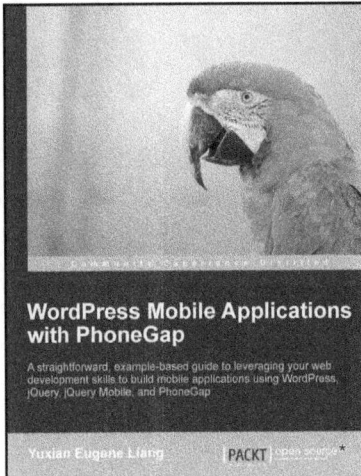

WordPress Mobile Applications with PhoneGap

ISBN: 978-1-84951-986-1   Paperback: 96 pages

A straightforward, example-based guide to leveraging your web develpoment skills to build mobile applications using WordPress, jQuery, jQuery Mobile, and PhoneGap

1. Discover how we can leverage on Wordpress as a content management system and serve content to mobile apps by exposing its API

2. Learn how to build geolocation mobile applications using Wordpress and PhoneGap

3. Step-by-step instructions on how you can make use of jQuery and jQuery mobile to provide an interface between Wordpress and your PhoneGap app.

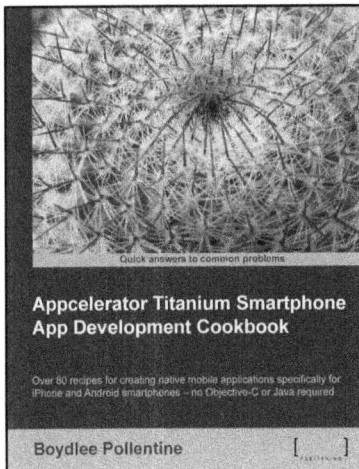

WordPress Mobile Applications with PhoneGap

A straightforward, example-based guide to leveraging your web development skills to build mobile applications using WordPress, jQuery, jQuery Mobile, and PhoneGap

Yuxian Eugene Liang

Appcelerator Titanium Smartphone App Development Cookbook

ISBN: 978-1-84951-396-8   Paperback: 308 pages

Over 80 recipes for creating native mobile applications specifically for iPhone and Android smartphones - no Objective-C or Java required

1. Leverage your JavaScript skills to write mobile applications using Titanium Studio tools with the native advantage!

2. Extend the Titanium platform with your own native modules

3. A practical guide for packaging and submitting your apps to both the iTunes store and Android Marketplace

Appcelerator Titanium Smartphone App Development Cookbook

Over 80 recipes for creating native mobile applications specifically for iPhone and Android smartphones – no Objective-C or Java required

Boydlee Pollentine

Please check **www.PacktPub.com** for information on our titles